Air fryer Cookbook Complete Edition 2021

Healthy and Fast Recipes for Smart People on a Budget | How to Fry, Grill, Bake, and Roast Your Favourite Meals

TASHA MANN

TABLE OF CONTENTS

Introduction

With technology giving birth to different and unique inventions every day to satisfy the hunger for innovation in society, the everyday kitchen's modernization is also seen. Among the many devices that have made life more comfortable with their usefulness and design, the Air Fryer is an excellent tool with many benefits.

An Air Fryer is a device that cooks food not by using oil but by heated air with no compromise on the dish's texture and flavor. Air Fryer is not only used for frying up food, but can also be used for many other tasks such as grilling, baking, roasting, and many more. It ensures the food is cooked evenly and thoroughly. Its design is such that it fits in a compact area and works via electricity. It has many different parts:

The frying basket: It is a stainless-steel basket in which the food is placed for cooking. It can be replaced by any other utensils, such as a pizza pan.

The timer: The timer is set accordingly; a red light indicates when the time has been finished.

The temperature controller: The temperature of the Air Fryer has a high range from 175 to 400F. Adjust the temp knob to achieve the desired temperature.

The air inlet/outlet: It is used to release the hot air and steam that arises during the cooking process from the device's back. It is, therefore, important that the device is always kept in a spacious area.

How to Start Cooking in An Air Fryer?

Firstly, the Air Fryer must be in a spacious place to allow heat to escape and prevent damage to its parts. It should be put on top of a heat resistance surface.

Secondly, pull out the frying basket gently from the machine. It is recommended to preheat the device for 5 minutes before using it. Simply set the desired temperature for 5 mins and then after the time is completed, pull out the basket.

Now place the food inside the container. Not more than 2/3 of the container should be filled. If required, the container can be greased with an oil spray to avoid sticking the food. If fatty foods are placed, add a little bit of water so that the container remains clean.

CHAPTER 1

Breakfast

1.   Mini Shrimp Frittata

Preparation Time: 15 minutesCooking Time: 20 minutes

Servings: 4

Ingredients:

1 teaspoon olive oil, plus more for spraying

½ small red bell pepper, finely diced

1 teaspoon minced garlic

1 (4-ounce) can of tiny shrimp, drained

Salt Freshly ground black pepper

4 eggs, beaten

4 teaspoons ricotta cheese

Directions:

Spray four ramekins with olive oil. In a medium skillet over medium-low heat, heat 1 teaspoon of olive oil. Add the bell pepper and garlic and sauté until the pepper is soft, about 5 minutes. Add the shrimp, season it with pepper and salt, and cook until warm, 1 to 2 minutes. Remove from the heat.

Add the eggs and stir to combine. Pour one quarter of the mixture into each ramekin. Place 2 ramekins in the fryer basket and cook for 6 minutes. Remove the fryer basket from the air fryer and stir the mixture in each ramekin. Top each fritatta with 1 teaspoon of ricotta cheese. Return the fryer basket to the air fryer and cook until eggs are set and the top is lightly browned, 4 to 5 minutes. Repeat with the remaining two ramekins. Note: the temperature of the air fryer should be 350°F.

Nutrition:

Calories 114 Fat 7g Carbohydrates 1g Protein 12g

2.   Spinach and Mushroom Mini Quiche

Preparation Time: 10 minutes

Cooking Time: 15 minutes

Servings: 4

Ingredients:

1 teaspoon olive oil, plus more for spraying

1 cup coarsely chopped mushrooms

1 cup fresh baby spinach, shredded

4 eggs, beaten

½ cup shredded Cheddar cheese

½ cup shredded mozzarella cheese

¼ teaspoon salt

¼ teaspoon black pepper

Directions:

Spray 4 silicone baking cups with olive oil and set aside. In a medium sauté pan over medium heat, warm 1 teaspoon of olive oil. Add the mushrooms and sauté until soft, 3 to 4 minutes.

Add the spinach and cook until wilted, 1 to 2 minutes. Set aside. In a medium bowl, whisk together the eggs, Cheddar cheese, mozzarella cheese, salt, and pepper. Gently fold the mushrooms and spinach into the egg mixture. Pour ¼ of the mixture into each silicone baking cup. Place the baking cups into the fryer basket and air fry for 5 minutes. Stir the mixture in each ramekin slightly and air fry until the egg has set, an additional 3 to 5 minutes.

Note: the temperature of the air fryer should be 350°F.

Nutrition:

Calories 183

Fat 13g

Carbohydrates 3g

Protein 14g

3.   Italian Egg Cups

Preparation Time: 5 minutes

Cooking Time: 10 minutes

Servings: 4

Ingredients:

Olive oil

1 cup marinara sauce

4 eggs

4 tablespoons shredded mozzarella cheese

4 teaspoons grated Parmesan cheese

Salt

Freshly ground black pepper

Chopped fresh basil, for garnish

Directions:

Lightly spray 4 individual ramekins with olive oil. Pour ¼ cup of marinara sauce into each ramekin. Crack one egg into each ramekin on top of the marinara sauce. Sprinkle 1 tablespoon

14

of mozzarella and 1 tablespoon of Parmesan on top of each egg. Season it with pepper and salt.

Cover each ramekin with aluminium foil. Place two of the ramekins in the fryer basket. Air fry for 5 minutes and remove the aluminium foil. Air fry it until the top is lightly browned and the egg white is cooked, another 2 to 4 minutes. If you prefer the yolk to be firmer, cook for 3 to 5 more minutes. Repeat with the remaining two ramekins. Garnish with basil and serve.

Note: the temperature of the air fryer should be 350°F.

Nutrition:

Calories 135

Fat 8g

Carbohydrates 6g

Protein 10g

4.   Mexican Breakfast Pepper Rings

Preparation Time: 5 minutes

Cooking Time: 10 minutes

Servings: 4

Ingredients:

Olive oil

1 large red, yellow, or orange bell pepper, cut into four ¾-inch rings

4 eggs

Salt

Freshly ground black pepper

2 teaspoons salsa

Directions:

Lightly spray a small round air fryer–friendly pan with olive oil. Place 2 bell pepper rings on the pan. Crack one egg into each bell pepper ring. Season with salt and black pepper. Spoon ½ teaspoon of salsa on top of each egg. Place the pan in the fryer basket. Air fry until the yolk is slightly runny, 5 to 6 minutes or until the yolk is fully cooked, 8 to 10 minutes. Repeat with the remaining 2 pepper rings. Serve hot.

Note: the temperature of the air fryer should be 350°F.

Pair It With: Turkey sausage or turkey bacon make this a heartier morning meal.

Air Fry Like a Pro: Use a silicone spatula to easily move the rings from the pan to your plate.

Nutrition:

Calories 84

Fat 5g

Carbohydrates: 3g

Protein 7g

5.　Cajun Breakfast Muffins

Preparation Time: 10 minutes

Cooking Time: 10 minutes

Servings: 6

Ingredients:

Olive oil

4 eggs, beaten

2¼ cups frozen hash browns, thawed

1 cup diced ham

½ cup shredded Cheddar cheese

½ teaspoon Cajun seasoning

Directions:

Lightly spray 12 silicone muffin cups with olive oil. In a medium bowl, mix together the eggs, hash browns, ham, Cheddar cheese, and Cajun seasoning in a medium bowl. Spoon a heaping 1½ tablespoons of hash brown mixture into each muffin cup. Place the muffin cups in the fryer basket.

Air fry until the muffins are golden brown on top and the center has set up, 8 to 10 minutes.

Note: the temperature of the air fryer should be 350°F.

Nutrition:

Calories 178

Fat 9g

Carbohydrates 13g

Protein 11g

6.   **Hearty Blueberry Oatmeal**

Preparation Time: 10 minutes

Cooking Time: 25 minutes

Servings: 6

Ingredients:

1½ cups quick oats

1¼ teaspoons ground cinnamon, divided

½ teaspoon baking powder

Pinch salt

1 cup unsweetened vanilla almond milk

¼ cup honey

1 teaspoon vanilla extract 1 egg, beaten

2 cups blueberries Olive oil 1½ teapoons sugar, divided

6 tablespoons low-fat whipped topping (optional)

Directions:

In a large bowl, mix together the oats, 1 teaspoon of cinnamon, baking powder, and salt. In a medium bowl, whisk together the almond milk, honey, vanilla and egg. Pour the liquid ingredients into the oats mixture and stir to combine. Fold in the blueberries.

Lightly spray a round air fryer–friendly pan with oil. Add half the blueberry mixture to the pan. Sprinkle ⅛ teaspoon of cinnamon and ½ teaspoon sugar over the top. Cover the pan with aluminum foil and place gently in the fryer basket. Air fry for 20 minutes. Remove the foil and air fry for an additional 5 minutes. Transfer the mixture to a shallow bowl. Repeat with the remaining blueberry mixture, ½ teaspoon of sugar, and ⅛ teaspoon of cinnamon. To serve, spoon into bowls and top with whipped topping.

Note: the temperature of the air fryer should be 360°F.

Nutrition:

Calories 170

Fat 3g Carbohydrates 34g

Protein 4g

7.   Banana Bread Pudding

Preparation Time: 10 minutes

Cooking Time: 10 minutes

Servings: 6

Ingredients:

Olive oil

2 medium ripe bananas, mashed

½ cup low-fat milk

2 tablespoons peanut butter

2 tablespoons maple syrup

1 teaspoon ground cinnamon

1 teaspoon vanilla extract

2 slices whole-grain bread, torn into bite-sized pieces

¼ cup quick oats

Directions:

Lightly spray four individual ramekins or one air fryer–safe

baking dish with olive oil. In a large mixing bowl, combine

the bananas, milk, peanut butter, maple syrup, cinnamon, and vanilla. Using an electric mixer or whisk, mix until fully combined. Add the bread pieces and stir to coat in the liquid mixture.

Add the oats and stir until everything is combined Transfer the mixture to the baking dish or divide between the ramekins. Cover with aluminium foil. Place 2 ramekins in the fryer basket and air fry until heated through, 10 to 12 minutes. Remove the foil and cook for 6 to 8 more minutes. Repeat with the remaining 2 ramekins.

Note: the temperature of the air fryer should be 350°F.

Nutrition:

Calories 212 Fat 6g Carbohydrates 38g

Protein 6g

CHAPTER 2

Mains

8.   Country Fried Steak

Preparation Time: 10 minutes

Cooking Time:15 minutes

Servings:2

Ingredients:

1 teaspoon pepper

2 C. almond milk

2 tablespoon almond flour

6 ounces ground sausage meat

1 teaspoon pepper

1 teaspoon salt

1 teaspoon garlic powder

1 teaspoon onion powder

1 C. panko breadcrumbs 1 C. almond flour 3 beaten eggs

6 ounces sirloin steak, pounded till thin

Directions:

Season panko breadcrumbs with spices. Dredge steak in flour, then egg, and then seasoned panko mixture. Place into air fryer basket. Cook 12 minutes at 370 degrees. To make sausage gravy, cook sausage and drain off fat, but reserve 2 tablespoons.

Add flour to sausage and mix until incorporated. Gradually mix in milk over medium to high heat till it becomes thick. Season mixture with pepper and cook 3 minutes longer. Serve steak topped with gravy and enjoy!

Nutrition:

Calories 395 Fat 11g Protein 39g ugar 5g

9.   Air Fryer Roast Beef

Preparation Time: 10 minutes

Cooking Time:45 minutes

Servings:6-8

Ingredients:

Roast beef

1 tablespoon olive oil

Seasonings of choice

Directions:

Ensure your air fryer is preheated to 160 degrees. Place roast in bowl and toss with olive oil and desired seasonings. Put seasoned roast into air fryer and cook 30 minutes. Turn roast when the timer sounds and cook another 15 minutes.

Nutrition:

Calories 267

Fat 8g Protein 21g

Sugar 1g

10. Crispy Mongolian Beef

Preparation Time: 10 minutes

Cooking Time:12 minutes

Servings:6-10

Ingredients:

Olive oil

½ cup almond flour

2 pounds beef tenderloin or beef chuck, sliced into strips

Sauce:

½ cup chopped green onion

1 teaspoon red chili flakes

1 teaspoon almond flour

½ cup brown sugar

1 teaspoon hoisin sauce

½ cup water

½ cup rice vinegar

½ cup low-sodium soy sauce

1 tablespoon chopped garlic

1 tablespoon finely chopped ginger

2 tablespoon olive oil

Directions:

Toss strips of beef in almond flour, ensuring they are coated well. Add to air fryer and cook 10 minutes at 300 degrees. Meanwhile, add all sauce ingredients to the pan and bring to a boil. Mix well.

Add beef strips to the sauce and cook 2 minutes. Serve over cauliflower rice!

Nutrition:

Calories 290

Fat 14g

Protein 22g

Sugar 1g

11.   Beef Taco Fried Egg Rolls

Preparation Time: 15 minutes

Cooking Time:12 minutes

Servings: 8

Ingredients:

1 teaspoon cilantro

2 chopped garlic cloves

1 tablespoon olive oil

1 cup shredded Mexican cheese

½ packet taco seasoning

½ can cilantro lime rotel

½ chopped onion

16 egg roll wrappers

1 pound lean ground beef

Directions:

Ensure that your air fryer is preheated to 400 degrees. Add onions and garlic to a skillet, cooking till fragrant. Then add taco seasoning, pepper, salt, and beef, cooking till beef is broke up into tiny pieces and cooked thoroughly. Add rotel and stir well.

Lay out egg wrappers and brush with water to soften a bit. Load wrappers with beef filling and add cheese to each. Fold diagonally to close and use water to secure edges.

Brush filled egg wrappers with olive oil and add to the air fryer. Cook 8 minutes, flip, and cook another 4 minutes. Served sprinkled with cilantro.

Nutrition:

Calories 348

Fat 11g

Protein 24g

Sugar 1g

12.   Pub Style Corned Beef Egg Rolls

Preparation Time: 5 minutes

Cooking Time:20 minutes

Servings:10

Ingredients:

Olive oil

½ cup orange marmalade

5 slices of Swiss cheese

4 cup corned beef and cabbage

1 egg

10 egg roll wrappers

Brandy Mustard Sauce:

1/16th teaspoon pepper

2 tablespoon whole grain mustard

1 teaspoon dry mustard powder

1 cup heavy cream

½ cup chicken stock

¼ cup brandy

¾ cup dry white wine

¼ teaspoon curry powder

½ tablespoon cilantro

1 minced shallot

2 tablespoon ghee

Directions:

To make mustard sauce, add shallots and ghee to skillet, cooking until softened. Then add brandy and wine, heating to a low boil. Cook 5 minutes for liquids to reduce. Add stock and seasonings. Simmer 5 minutes.

Turn down heat and add heavy cream. Cook on low till sauce reduces and it covers the back of a spoon. Place sauce in the fridge to chill.

Crack the egg in a bowl and set to the side. Lay out an egg wrapper with the corner towards you. Brush the edges with egg wash.

Place 1/3 cup of corned beef mixture into the center along with 2 tablespoons of marmalade and ½ a slice of Swiss cheese. Fold the bottom corner over filling. As you are folding the sides, make sure they are stick well to the first flap you made.

Place filled rolls into prepared air fryer basket. Spritz rolls with olive oil. Cook 10 minutes at 390 degrees, shaking halfway through cooking.

Serve rolls with Brandy Mustard sauce and devour!

Nutrition:

Calories 415 Fat 13g Protein 38g Sugar 4g

CHAPTER 3

Sides

13.   Beef Roll-Ups

Preparation Time: 5 minutes

Cooking Time: 10 minutes

Servings: 4

Ingredients:

2 lb. beef flank steak

3 tbsp pesto

.75 cup fresh baby spinach

3 oz. roasted red bell peppers

6 slices provolone cheese

Pepper & sea salt

Directions:

Heat the Air Fryer to 400° Fahrenheit. Slice the steak open (not all the way through) to spread the pesto over the meat. Layer the peppers, cheese, and spinach (about ¾ of the way into the meat). Roll it up with toothpicks. Give it a sprinkle of pepper and salt. Set the timer for 4 minutes – rotating halfway through the cycle. When it's done, wait for about 10 minutes before slicing to serve.

Nutrition:

Calories 125

Fat 13g

Protein 15g

14.   Beef & Bacon Taco Rolls

Preparation Time: 5 minutes

Cooking Time: 15 minutes

Servings: 4

Ingredients:

2 cups ground beef

.5 cups bacon bits

1 cup tomato salsa

4 turmeric coconut wraps/your choice

1 cup shredded Monterey Jack Cheese

To Your Liking - The Spices:

Garlic powder

Chili powder

Black pepper

Direction

Warm the fryer to reach 390° Fahrenheit. Add all of the spice

fixings together and toss with the beef. Prepare and roll the wraps and place in the Air Fryer. Set the timer for 15 minutes and serve.

Nutrition:

Calories 450 Fat 23g Protein 11g

15. Chicken Kabobs

Preparation Time: 5 minutes

Cooking Time: 10 minutes

Servings: 2

Ingredients

3 bell peppers – multi colors of your choice

6 mushrooms

.33 cup soy sauce

.33 cup honey

Pepper and salt

Sesame seeds

2 chicken breasts

Cooking oil spray

Directions:

Dice the chicken and peppers. Chop the mushrooms into halves. Give the chicken a couple of squirts of oil and a pinch of salt and pepper. Combine the soy and honey – mixing well.

Add sesame seeds and stir. Insert the peppers, chicken, and mushroom bits onto a skewer. Set the temperature of the Air Fryer to 338° Fahrenheit. Cover the kabobs with the sauce and arrange them in the fryer basket. Set the timer for 15-20 minutes and serve.

Nutrition:

Calories 230

Fat 13.4g

Protein 11g

16.   Crispy Gnocchi

Preparation Time: 5 minutes

Cooking Time: 10 minutes

Servings: 4

Ingredients:

12 oz. frozen gnocchi

 2 tbsp vegetable/olive oil

3 tbsp parmesan cheese

Direction

Set the Air Fryer temp to 350° Fahrenheit for one to two minutes. Add the gnocchi into a bowl and toss it with oil (not coconut oil). Toss the gnocchi in the fryer and fry for 8 to 10 minutes until they're starting to turn golden brown.

Toss the fixings in the basket every few minutes to allow even cooking. Remove the gnocchi from the Air Fryer and place it on a serving tray.

Lightly mist the tops with a spritz of oil if desired and a sprinkle of parmesan cheese. Serve immediately with marinara on the side as a dipping sauce.

Nutrition:

Calories 310

Fat 12g

Protein 16g

17. Mac "N" Cheese Balls

Preparation Time: 5 minutes

Cooking Time: 10 minutes

Servings: 5

Ingredients:

2 cups macaroni and cheese

.33 cup Shredded cheddar cheese

3 eggs

2 cups milk

.75 cup white flour

1 cup plain bread crumbs

Directions:

Set the temperature of the Air Fryer to 360° Fahrenheit. Combine the leftovers with the shredded cheese. Place the breadcrumbs into a dish. Measure the flour into another bowl. Combine the milk and eggs. Prepare a small-sized ball from the macaroni and cheese. Roll the balls in the flour, eggs, and lastly the breadcrumbs. Place the balls in the fryer basket. Select the chicken icon. Set the timer for 10 minutes rotating halfway through the cooking cycle. Serve as a snack or delicious side dish.

Nutrition:

Calories 332

Fat 13g

Protein 7g

18.   **Meatballs For The Party**

Preparation Time: 5 minutes

Cooking Time: 15 minutes

Servings: 24

Ingredients:

2.5 tbsp Worcestershire sauce

1 lb. ground beef

1 tbsp Tabasco sauce

 1 tbsp lemon juice

.75 cup tomato ketchup

.25 vinegar

5 .tsp dry mustard

.5 cup brown sugar

3 crushed gingersnaps

Directions:

Combine all of the seasonings in a large mixing container—

blending well. Mix the beef and continue churning the

ingredients. Make the balls and arrange them in the Air Fryer. Cook at 375° Fahrenheit for 15 minutes. They're ready when the center is done. Place them on toothpicks before serving.

Nutrition:

Calories 224.3

Fat 22g

Protein 9g

19.   Mini Bacon-Wrapped Burritos (Vegan)

Preparation Time: 5 minutes

Cooking Time: 10 minutes

Servings: 4

Ingredients:

2 tbsp water

2 Tofu Scramble or Vegan Egg

3 tbsp Tamari

2 tbsp cashew butter

2 tbsp liquid smoke

4 rice paper

Vegetable Add-Ins:

8 roasted red pepper

.33 cup sweet potato roasted cubes

1 small sautéed tree broccoli

1 small green

8 stalks fresh asparagus

Directions

Preheat the Air Fryer to 350° Fahrenheit. Preparing a baking pan with parchment baking paper to fit inside the fryer. Whisk the cashew butter, water, tamari, and liquid smoke. Set it aside for now. Preparingthe Filling: Hold a rice paper under cold running water to get both sides wet. Place on the plate to fill. Start by filling the fixings –just off from the center—leaving the sides of the paper open. Fold in two of the sides to make the burrito.

Seal and dip each one in the liquid smoke mixture—coating completely. Cook until crispy (8-10 min.). Serve when ready.

Nutrition:

Calories 340

Fat 16g

Protein 12g

20.   Mozzarella Sticks

Preparation Time: 5 minutes

Cooking Time: 12 minutes

Servings: 4

Ingredients:

2 eggs

1 lb.Mozzarella cheese

1 cup plain bread crumbs

.25 cupwhite flour

3 tbsp nonfat milk

Directions:

Set the temperature of the Air Fryer to 400° Fahrenheit. Slice the cheese into ½-inch by 3-inch sticks. Whisk the milk and eggs together in one bowl, with the oil and breadcrumbs in individual dishes as well. Dredge the sliced cheese through the oil, egg, and breadcrumbs. Place the sticks onto a bread tray and put them in the freezer compartment for about an hour or two. Arrange them in small increments into the fryer basket. Cook for 12 minutes.

Nutrition:

Calories 245

Fat 13.6g

Protein 12g

CHAPTER 4

Fish and Seafood

21.   Tuna Stuffed Potatoes

Preparation Time: 15 minutes

Cooking Time: 30 minutes

Servings: 4

Ingredients:

1½-pounds tuna, drained

2 tablespoons plain Greek yogurt

½ tablespoon olive oil

4 starchy potatoes, soaked for 30 minutes

1 tablespoon capers

1 teaspoon red chili powder

1 scallion, chopped and divided

Salt and freshly ground black pepper, to taste

Directions:

Preheat the air fryer to 355 degrees F.

Place the potatoes in the air fryer basket and cook for about 30 minutes.

Take out and place on a flat surface.

Meanwhile, add yogurt, tuna, red chili powder, scallion, salt and pepper in a bowl. Mix well.

Cut each potato from top side lengthwise and press the open side of potato halves slightly.

Stuff potato with tuna mixture and sprinkle with capers.

Dish out and serve.

Tip: Top with mint and oregano to enhance taste.

Nutrition:

Calories 1387 Fat 54g Carbs 35.7g Fiber 2.7g

Protein 180.7g

22. Packet Lobster Tail

Preparation Time: 27 minutes

Cooking Time: 12 minutes

Servings: 2

Ingredients:

2 (6-oz. lobster tails, halved

2 tbsp. salted butter; melted.

1 tsp. dried parsley.

½ tsp. Old Bay seasoning

Juice of ½ medium lemons

Directions:

Place the two halved tails on a sheet of aluminum foil. Drizzle

with butter, Old Bay seasoning and lemon juice.

Seal the foil packets, completely covering tails. Place into the

air fryer basket

Adjust the temperature to 375 Degrees F and set the timer for 12 minutes. Once done, sprinkle with dried parsley and serve immediately.

Nutrition:

Calories: 234 Protein: 23g

Fiber: 1g Fat: 19g Carbs: 7g

23. Parmesan Tilapia Fillets

Preparation Time: 7 minutes

Cooking Time: 15 minutes

Servings: 4

Ingredients:

¾ cup Parmesan cheese, grated

1 tbsp olive oil

1 tsp paprika

1 tbsp fresh parsley, chopped

¼ tsp garlic powder

¼ tsp salt

4 tilapia fillets

Directions

Preheat Beeville on Air fryer oven function to 350 F. In a bowl, mix parsley, Parmesan cheese, garlic, salt, and paprika. Coat in the tilapia fillets and place them in a lined baking sheet.

Drizzle with the olive oil press Start. Cook for 8-10 minutes until golden. Serve warm.

Nutrition:

Calories 345

Fat 1g

Protein 18g

Fiber 4g

24. Party Cod Nuggets

Preparation Time: 10 minutes

Cooking Time: 20 minutes

Servings: 4

Ingredients:

1 ¼ lb. cod fillets, cut into 4 chunks each

½ cup flour

1 egg

1 cup cornflakes

1 tbsp olive oil

Salt and black pepper to taste

Directions

Place the oil and cornflakes in a food processor and process until crumbed. Season the fish chunks with salt and pepper. In a bowl, beat the egg with 1 tbsp of water.

Dredge the chunks in flour first, then dip in the egg, and finally coat with cornflakes. Arrange on a lined sheet and press Start. Cook on an Air fryer oven function at 350 F for 15 minutes until crispy. Serve.

Nutrition:

Calories 165

Carbs 5.8

Fat 4.5g

Protein 24g

CHAPTER 5

Poultry

25. Boneless Turkey Breasts

Preparation Time: 10 minutes

Cooking Time: 60 minutes

Servings: 4

Ingredients:

4 lb. boneless turkey breast

1/4 cup mayo

2 tsp. poultry seasoning

1 tsp. salt

1/4 tsp. black pepper

1/2 tsp. garlic powder

Directions:

Preheat air fryer toaster oven to 380 degrees Fahrenheit.

Season the turkey breast with mayonnaise, poultry seasoning, salt, garlic powder, and black pepper.

Air fry on 360 degrees Fahrenheit for 1 hour or until internal temperature has reached a temperature of 165 degrees Fahrenheit.

Nutrition:

Calories: 152

Fat: 5g

Protein: 25g

Carbs: 1g

26. Juicy Chicken Thighs

Preparation Time: 5 minutes

Cooking Time: 20 minutes

Servings: 4

Ingredients:

1/2 tsp. salt

1/2 tsp. smoked paprika

1/2 tsp. oregano

1/2 tsp. cumin

1 tsp. brown sugar

1/4 tsp. pepper

4 boneless skinless chicken thighs

Directions:

Combine together the chicken seasonings and then sprinkle on the top and bottom of your chicken thighs.

Put the chicken thighs in the air fryer for 20 mins at 350 degrees F or until the thickest part of the chicken reaches 165 degrees F.

Nutrition:

Calories: 142

Fat: 4g

Protein: 21g

Carbs: 1g

Fiber: 1g

27. Garlic Parmesan Chicken Tender

Preparation Time: 5 minutes

Cooking Time: 12 minutes Servings: 4

Ingredients:

8 chicken tenders

1 egg

Cooking spray

1/2 tsp. salt

1 tsp. garlic powder

1/4 tsp. black pepper

1/2 tsp. onion powder

1 cup dipping sauce

1 cup panko breadcrumbs 1/4 cup parmesan cheese

Directions:

Mix the dredge coating ingredients in a bowl or baking pan to fit the chicken pieces. In a second bowl or baking pan, put egg and water and whisk to mix.

Dip the chicken tenders into the egg wash and then into the panko dredge mixture.

Put the breaded tenders into the fry basket. Do same with remaining tenders.

Spray a light coat of olive oil or non-fat cooking spray over the panko. Now set the temperature to 400 degrees and fry for 12 minutes.

The cooking time may be more or less depending on the size and thickness of your chicken tenders, fingers or nuggets, and the quantity of chicken in the basket.

Nutrition:

Calories: 220

Fat: 6g

Protein: 27g

Carbs: 13g

Fiber: 1g

28. Chicken Meatballs

Preparation Time: 5 minutes

Cooking Time: 15 minutes

Servings: 2

Ingredients:

½ lb. chicken breast

1 tbsp of garlic

1 tbsp of onion

½ chicken broth

1 tbsp of oatmeal, whole wheat flour or of your choice

1 pinch of paprika

Salt and black pepper

Directions:

Place all of the ingredients in a food processor and beat well until well mixed and ground.

If you don't have a food processor, ask the butcher to grind it and then add the other ingredients, mixing well.

Make balls and place them in the Air Fryer basket.

Program the Air Fryer for 15 minutes at 400ºF.

Half the time shake the basket so that the meatballs loosen and fry evenly.

Nutrition:

Calories: 45

Carbohydrates: 1.94g

Fat: 1.57g

Protein: 5.43g

Sugar: 0.41g

Cholesterol: 23m

29. Rolled Turkey Breast

Preparation Time: 5 minutes

Cooking Time: 10 minutes

Servings: 4

Ingredients:

1 box of cherry tomatoes

¼ lb. turkey blanket

Directions:

Wrap the turkey and blanket in the tomatoes, close with the help of toothpicks.

Take to Air Fryer for 10 minutes at 390F.

You can increase the filling with ricotta and other preferred light ingredients.

Nutrition:

Calories: 172 Carbohydrates: 3g

Fat: 2g Protein: 34g

Sugar: 1g Cholesterol: 300mg

30.   Chicken Hash

Preparation Time: 5 minutes

Cooking Time: 14 minu Servings: 3

Ingredients:

6-ounces of cauliflower, chopped

7-ounce chicken fillet

1 tablespoon water

1 green pepper, chopped

½ yellow onion, diced

1 teaspoon ground black pepper

3 tablespoons butter

1 tablespoon cream

Directions:

Chop the cauliflower and place into the blender and blend it carefully until you get cauliflower rice. Chop the chicken fillet into small pieces. Sprinkle the chicken fillet with ground black pepper and stir.   Preheat your air fryer to

380°Fahrenheit. Dice the yellow onion and chop the green pepper. In a large mixing bowl, combine ingredients, and then add mixture to fryer basket. Then cook and serve chicken hash warm!

Nutrition:

Calories: 261

Fat: 16.8g

Carbs: 7.1g

Protein: 21g

CHAPTER 6

Meat

31. Bacon, Lettuce, Tempeh & Tomato Sandwiches

Preparation Time: 5 minutes

Cooking Time: 5 minutes

Servings: 4

Ingredients:

8-ounce package tempeh

1 cup warm vegetable broth

Tomato slices and lettuce, to serve

¼ teaspoon chipotle chili powder

½ teaspoon garlic powder

½ teaspoon onion powder

1 teaspoon Liquid smoke

3 tablespoons soy sauce

Directions:

Begin by opening the packet of tempeh and slice into pieces about ¼ inch thick. Grab a medium bowl and add the remaining ingredients except for lettuce and tomato and stir well. Place the pieces of tempeh onto a baking tray that will fit into your air fryer and pour over the flavor mix.

Put the tray in air fryer and cook for 5-minutes at 360°Fahrenheit. Remove from air fryer and place on sliced bread with the tomato and lettuce and any other extra toppings you desire.

Nutrition: Carbs: 265

Fat: 11.3g

Carbs: 9.2g

Protein: 12.4g

32. Chinese Pork Roast

Preparation: 5 minutesCooking: 15 minutes Servings: 4

Ingredients:

2 lbs. pork shoulder, chopped

½ tablespoon salt

1/3 cup soy sauce

1 tablespoon honey

1 tablespoon liquid Stevia

Directions:

Place all the ingredients into a mixing bowl and combine well. Place marinated pork in fridge for 2-hours. Spray air fryer basket with cooking spray. Add marinated pork pieces into air fryer basket and cook at 350°Fahrenheit for 10-minutes. Now increase temperature to 400°Fahrenheit and cook for an additional 5-minutes.

Nutrition:Calories: 283 Total Fat: 12.3g

Carbs: 11.5g Protein: 16.7g

33.   Sweet & Sour Pork

Preparation Time: 10 minutes

Cooking Time: 22 minutes

Servings: 4

Ingredients:

¾ lb. pork, chunked

1 slice of pineapple, cut into pieces

1 medium tomato, chopped

2 tablespoons oyster sauce

2 tablespoons tomato sauce

1 tablespoon Worcestershire sauce

1 medium onion, sliced

1 tablespoon garlic, minced

1 teaspoon olive oil

Almond flour

1 egg, beaten

1 tablespoon liquid Stevia

Directions:

Preheat the air fryer to 250°Fahrenheit for 5-minutes. Dip pork pieces in egg then coat with flour and place into an air fryer basket. Air fry pork pieces in a preheated air fryer for 20-minutes. Heat oil in a pan over medium heat. Add onion and garlic into pan and sauté for 2-minutes. Place all remaining ingredients into the pan and stir. Add pork to the pan and stir well. Serve hot!

Nutrition:

Calories: 286,

Fat: 12.5g,

Carbs: 11.6g,

Protein: 16.3g

34. Simple Beef Patties

Preparation Time: 10 minutes

Cooking Time: 13 minutes

Servings: 4

Ingredients:

1 lb ground beef

½ tsp garlic powder

¼ tsp onion powder

Pepper

Salt

Directions:

Preheat the instant vortex air fryer oven to 400 F.

Add ground meat, garlic powder, onion powder, pepper, and salt into the mixing bowl and mix until well combined.

Make even shape patties from meat mixture and arrange on air fryer pan.

Place pan in instant vortex air fryer oven.

Cook patties for 10 minutes. Turn patties after 5 minutes.

Serve and enjoy.

Nutrition:

Calories 212

Fat 7.1 g

Carbohydrates 0.4 g

Cholesterol 101 mg

35. Marinated Pork Chops

Preparation Time: 10 minutes

Cooking Time: 30 minutes

Servings: 2

Ingredients:

2 pork chops, boneless

1 tsp garlic powder

½ cup flour

1 cup buttermilk

Pepper

Salt

Directions:

Add pork chops and buttermilk in a zip-lock bag. Seal the bag and place in the refrigerator overnight.

In another zip-lock bag add flour, garlic powder, pepper, and salt.

Remove marinated pork chops from buttermilk and add in flour mixture and shake until well coated.

Preheat the instant vortex air fryer oven to 380 F.

Spray air fryer tray with cooking spray.

Arrange pork chops on a tray and air fryer for 28-30 minutes.

Turn pork chops after 18 minutes.

Serve and enjoy.

Nutrition:

Calories 424

Fat 21.3 g

Carbohydrates 30.8 g

Sugar 6.3 g

Protein 25.5 g

Cholesterol 74 mg

36. Smoked Beef Burgers

Preparation Time: 10 minutes

Cooking Time: 10 minutes

Servings: 4

Ingredients:

1 ¼ pounds lean ground beef

1 tablespoon soy sauce

1 teaspoon Dijon mustard

A few dashes of liquid smoke

1 teaspoon shallot powder

1 clove garlic, minced

1/2 teaspoon cumin powder

1/4 cup scallions, minced

1/3 teaspoon sea salt flakes

1/3 teaspoon freshly cracked mixed peppercorns

1 teaspoon celery seeds

1 teaspoon parsley flakes

Directions:

Mix all of the above ingredients in a bowl; knead until everything is well incorporated.

Shape the mixture into four patties. Next, make a shallow dip in the center of each patty to prevent them puffing up during air-frying.

Spritz the patties on all sides using a non-stick cooking spray.

Cook approximately 12 minutes at 360 degrees F.

Check for doneness – an instant read thermometer should read 160 degrees F. Bon appétit!

Nutrition:

167 Calories

5.5g Fat

1.4g Carbs

26.4g Protein

0g Sugars

0.4g Fiber

CHAPTER 7

Vegetables

37.   Beet Salad and Parsley Dressing

Preparation Time: 5 minutes

Cooking Time: 14 minutes

Servings: 4

Ingredients:

4 beets

 2 tbsp. balsamic vinegar

1 bunch parsley chopped

salt and black pepper to taste

1 tbsp. extra-virgin olive oil –

1 cloves garlic chopped

2 tbsps capers

Directions:

Put beets in the air fryer and cook at 360F for 14 minutes. Meanwhile, in a bowl, mix garlic, parsley, olive oil, salt, pepper, and capers and mix well. Remove the beets, and cool. Peel and slice them. Add vinegar, drizzle the parsley dressing over and serve.

Nutrition:

Calories 70

 Fat 2g

Protein 4g

38. Cauliflower and Broccoli Delight

Preparation Time: 10 minutes

Cooking Time: 7 minutes

Servings: 4

Ingredients:

2 cauliflower heads, florets separated and steamed

1 broccoli head, florets separated and steamed

zest from 1 orange, grated

Juice from 1 orange

A pinch of hot pepper flakes

4 anchovies

1 tbsp. capers, chopped

salt and black pepper to the taste

4 tbsp. olive oil

Directions:

In a bowl, mix orange zest with orange juice, pepper flakes, anchovies, capers salt, pepper and olive oil and whisk well.

Add broccoli and cauliflower, toss well, transfer them to your air fryer's basket and cook at 400 degrees F for 7 minutes. Divide among plates and serve as a side dish with some of the orange vinaigrette drizzled on top.

Enjoy!

Nutrition:

Calories 300

Fat 4g

Protein 4g

39. Garlic Beet Wedges

Preparation Time: 10 minutes

Cooking Time: 15 minutes

Servings: 4

Ingredients:

4 beets, washed, peeled and cut into large wedges

1 tbsp. olive oil

salt and black to the taste

2 garlic cloves, minced

1 tsp. lemon juice

Directions:

In a bowl, mix beets with oil, salt, pepper, garlic and lemon juice, toss well, transfer to your air fryer's basket and cook them at 400 degrees F for 15 minutes. Divide beets wedges on plates and serve as a side dish. Enjoy!

Nutrition: Calories 182 Fat 6g

Protein 2g

40.   Fried Red Cabbage

Preparation Time: 10 minutes

Cooking Time: 15 minutes

Servings: 4

Ingredients:

4 garlic cloves, minced

½ cup yellow onion, chopped

1 tbsp. olive oil

6 cups red cabbage, chopped

1 cup veggie stock

1 tbsp. apple cider vinegar

1 cup applesauce

salt and black pepper to the taste

Directions:

In a heatproof dish that fits your air fryer, mix cabbage with onion, garlic, oil, stock, vinegar, applesauce, salt and pepper, toss really well, place the dish in your air fryer's basket and cook at 380 degrees F for 15 minutes. Divide among plates and serve as a side dish.

Enjoy!

Nutrition:

Calories 172

Fat 7g,

Protein 5g

CHAPTER 8

Soup and Stews

41.   English Pub Split Pea Soup

Preparation Time: 5 minutes

Cooking Time: 7 minutes

Servings: 4

Ingredients:

4 cups water

1 meaty ham bone

12-ounce light beer

1/4 tsp. pepper

1/2 tsp. salt

1/4 tsp. ground nutmeg

2 celery ribs, chopped

1 and a 1/3 cups dried green split peas

1 carrot, chopped

1 tbsp. English mustard

1 sweet onion, chopped

1/4 cup minced parsley

1/2 cup 2% milk

Directions:

Set the Air fryer oven on Roast to 365 degrees F for 7 minutes.

Put water, ham bone, beer, celery, peas, carrot, mustard and onion in the cooking tray.

Insert the cooking tray in the oven.

Remove from the oven when Cooking time is complete.

Serve warm.

Nutrition:

Calories 174 Protein 8.5g Carbohydrates 17.1g

Fat 10.4g

CHAPTER 9

Snacks

42.   Stewed Celery Stalk

Preparation Time: 10 minutes

Cooking Time:8 minutes Servings:6

Ingredients:

1-pound celery stalk

1 tablespoon butter

3 oz. chive stems, diced

1 cup chicken stock

2 tablespoons heavy cream

1 teaspoon salt

1 tablespoon paprika

Directions:

Chop the celery stalk roughly. Pour the chicken stock into the air fryer basket tray and add the diced chives. Preheat the air fryer to 400 F.

Cook the chives for 4 minutes. After this, reduce the heat to 365 F. Add the chopped celery stalk, butter, salt, paprika, and heavy cream.

Mix the vegetable mixture. Cook the celery for 8 minutes more. When the time is over – the celery stalk should be very soft.

Chill the side dish to the room temperature.

Serve it and enjoy!

Nutrition:

Calories 59, Fat 13,

Fiber 0.4, Carbs 1.5,

Protein 9.5

43. White Mushrooms with Spicy Cream

Preparation Time: 10 minutes

Cooking Time:12 minutes

Servings:4

Ingredients:

9 oz. white mushrooms

1 teaspoon garlic, sliced

3 oz. chive stems, sliced

1 cup cream

1 teaspoon butter

1 teaspoon olive oil

1 teaspoon ground red pepper

1 teaspoon chili flakes

Directions:

Slice the white mushrooms.

Sprinkle the white mushrooms with the chili flakes and ground red pepper.

Mix the mixture up.

After this, preheat the air fryer to 400 F.

Pour the olive oil in the air fryer basket tray.

Then add the sliced mushrooms and cook the vegetables for 5 minutes.

After this, add the sliced chives, cream, butter, sliced garlic, and mix the mushroom gently with the help of the spatula.

Cook the dish for 7 minutes at 365 F.

When the time is over – stir the side dish carefully.

Serve it warm.

Enjoy!

Nutrition:

Calories 98,

Fat 13,

Fiber 0.4,

Carbs 1.5,

Protein 9.5

CHAPTER 10

Desserts

44.   Corn Waffles

Preparation Time: 5 minutes

Cooking Time: 10 minutes Servings: 4

Ingredients:

1 ½ cups almond flour

3 eggs

2 tsp. dried basil

2 tsp. dried parsley

salt and pepper to taste

3 tbsp. butter

2 cups boiled corn and mayonnaise

Directions:

Preheat the air fryer to 250 F. In a small bowl, mix the ingredients, except the corn and mayo.

Take a waffle shape and grease it with butter. Pour the batter and cook till both sides have browned. Top with corn and mayo

Nutrition:

Calories 115 Fat 5.1g Protein 6.3g

45. Mixed Vegetable Muffins

Preparation Time: 5 minutes

Cooking Time: 15 minutes Servings: 4

Ingredients:

2 cups All-purpose flour

1 ½ cup milk

½ tsp. baking powder

½ tsp. baking soda

2 tbsp. butter

2 cups mixed vegetables

1 tbsp. sugar

muffin cups

Directions:

Mix the Ingredients: together and use your fingers to get a crumbly mixture. Add the baking soda to the milk and mix continuously. Add this milk to the mixture and create a batter, which you will need to transfer to the muffin cups. Preheat the fryer to 300 F for 5 minutes. You will need to place the muffin cups in the basket and cover it. Cook the muffins for 15 minutes and check whether or not the muffins are cooked using a toothpick. Remove the cups and serve hot.

Nutrition:

Calories 161

Fat 6.1g

Protein 4.8g

46. Vanilla Cupcakes

Preparation Time: 5 minutes

Cooking Time: 15 minutes

Servings: 4

Ingredients:

2 cups wheat flour

1 ½ cup milk

½ tsp. baking powder

½ tsp. baking soda

2 tbsp. butter

1 tbsp. honey

3 tbsp. vanilla extract

2 tsp. vinegar

muffin cups

Directions:

Combine the Ingredients: except milk to create a crumbly

blend. Add this milk to the blend and make a batter and pour into the muffin cups. Preheat the fryer to 300 F and cook for 15 minutes. Check whether they are done using a toothpick.

Nutrition:

Calories 161 Fat 5.6g Protein 7.2g

47. Pear Muffins

Preparation Time: 5 minutes

Cooking Time: 15 minutes

Servings: 4

Ingredients:

2 cups All-purpose flour

1 ½ cup buttermilk

½ tsp. baking powder

½ tsp. baking soda

2 tbsp. butter

2 tbsp. sugar

2 cups sliced pears

muffin cups

Directions:

Combine the ingredients, except milk to create a crumbly blend. Add this milk to the blend and make a batter and pour into the muffin cups. Preheat the fryer to 300 F and cook for 15 minutes. Check whether they are done using a toothpick.

Nutrition:

Calories 114 Fat 4.8g

Protein 6.1g

48. Air Fryer Brownies

Preparation Time: 10 minutes

Cooking Time: 30 minutes

Servings: 4

Ingredients:

1/4 cup non dairy milk

1/4 cup aquafaba

1/2 tsp vanilla extract

1/2 cup whole wheat flour

1/2 cup vegan sugar

1/4 cup cocoa powder

1 tbsp ground flax seeds

1/4 tsp salt

1/4 cup chopped hazelnuts and mini vegan chocolate chips

Directions:

Mix all dry ingredients Ingredients: in a bowl and wet Ingredients: in a large cup. Add wet and dry together and mix thoroughly. Fold in hazelnuts and chocolate chips. Preheat the air fryer to 175° C and line a baking pan with parchment paper. Place the pan in an air fryer basket and cook for 20 minutes or until a knife stuck in the middle comes out clean.

Nutrition:

Calories 248

Fat 8.2g

Protein 5.2g

49. Air Fryer Carrot Cake in a Mug

Preparation Time: 10 minutes

Cooking Time: 25 minutes

Servings: 1

Ingredients:

1 shredded carrot

1/4 cup whole wheat flour pastry

1 tbsp brown sugar

1/4 tsp of baking powder

1/4 tsp ground cinnamon

2 tbsp and 2 tsp non dairy milk

2 tbsp chopped walnuts

1 tbsp raisin

2 tsp oil pinch of ground allspice pinch of salt

Directions:

Oil an oven safe mug. Add flour, baking powder, cinnamon, ginger, allspice and salt, and mix together properly with a fork.

Add milk, carrots, walnuts, raisins and oil. Mix again. Air fry at 175°C for 15 minutes or until a fork inserted into the middle comes out clean. Serve and enjoy.

Nutrition:

Calories 151

Fat 5.7g

Protein 6.7g

50. The Heat Wave

Preparation Time: 5 minutes

Cooking Time: 10 minutes

Servings: 4

Ingredients:

1 cup plain flour

1 tbsp. unsalted butter

4tsp. powdered sugar

2 cups cold milk

Filling:

1 cup sliced pineapple

1 cup sliced papaya

2 tbsp. sugar ½ tsp. cinnamon 2 tsp. lemon juice

Directions:

Mix the first four ingredients: together to create a dough. Roll the batter out into 2 large circles. Press one circle into the pie tin and prick the sides with a fork. Cook the filling

Ingredients: over low heat and pour it in the tin. Cover the pie tin with the second circle. Preheat the fryer to 300 F for 5 minutes. Cook until golden brown, then let it cool. Slice and serve with a dab of cream.

Nutrition:

Calories 111

Fat 5.9g

Protein 4.3g

Conclusion

Unlike frying things in a typical pan on gas which fails to make your fries crisp and leaves your samosa uncooked due to uneven heat. The inbuilt kitchen deep fryers do it all; you can have perfectly crisp French fries like the one you get in restaurants. Your samosas will be perfectly cooked inside- out. Well, the list doesn't end here it goes on and on the potato wedges, chicken and much more. You can make many starters and dishes using fryer and relish the taste buds of your loved ones.

The new air fryers come along with a lot of features, so you don't mess up doing things enjoy your cooking experience. The free hot to set the temperature according to your convenience both mechanically and electronically. Oil filters to reuse the oil and use it for a long run. With the ventilation system to reduce and eliminate the frying odor. In a few models you also get the automatic timers and alarm set for convenient cooking, frying I mean. Also, the auto- push and raise feature to immerse or hold back the frying basket to achieve the perfect frying aim. So, why should you wait? I am sure you don't want to mess in your kitchen when grilling, baking of frying your food, right? Get yourself an air fryer. Thank you for purchasing this cookbook I hope you will apply all the acquired knowledge productively.

CPSIA information can be obtained
at www.ICGtesting.com
Printed in the USA
LVHW021526110521
687091LV00003B/558